Introduction for Teachers

 The Ocean

The ocean and its inhabitants have been a favorite course of study for students of all ages. Marine science, the study of the ocean, the creatures that live within, and the processes that shape it, holds a special wonder that sparks the imagination and stirs a sense of adventure. Since the ocean is not our natural home, it is not as familiar to us as many other topics of study – therein lies the wonder. Scientists have been studying the ocean and the animals that live within it for centuries, yet even today, in the age of technology, there are still regions of the ocean that we know little about and strange new species of animals that are yet to be discovered.

 About This Book

This book will allow teachers to guide young students through a series of scientific experiments and cross-curricular activities in marine science. A scientific background is not necessary. Information on all the topics is included so that teachers can introduce their classes to the activities without having to perform their own detailed research.

There are three books in this series, each designed for different grade levels. In addition, each book focuses on a different marine ecosystem:

- **Book 1** (grades K-2) - the tide pool
- **Book 2** (grades 3-5) - the kelp forest
- **Book 3** (grades 6-8) - the coral reef

While each book focuses on one particular ecosystem, the information and activities presented in each book encompass other areas of the ocean as well.

Each topic contains background information for teachers, experiments or activities and follow-up questions aimed at leading students into thinking critically about the activities.

Each activity or experiment is designed to stand alone or to be used in connection with others in a marine science unit. It may also be helpful to supplement these lessons with books or videos about the ocean from your school or public library. At the end of the book is a glossary, defining many of the scientific words used in the book. You may want to use these words as spelling or vocabulary words during the unit.

 Equipment

The equipment needed for each activity has been kept simple. Most items can be found in your classroom or at a local store. A list of scientific suppliers has also been included on page 4 in case you need to order any additional supplies. For some of the supplies, such as shoe boxes, it is often possible to have the students supply their own.

If You Can Visit the Ocean

If you live by the ocean, a field trip to a local tide pool or beach at the end of the marine science unit will give students a hands-on experience with the topics that they have been studying. At the end of each section you will find field study activities that can be done at the beach or in the classroom after a visit to the beach. Since student transportation is often difficult to arrange, check to see if you can legally collect items from the beach and bring them into the classroom. Some specimens can be collected without a permit in most states. It may also be possible, after obtaining a permit, to collect live specimens at the ocean and keep them in the classroom for the students to observe. Please check your local laws concerning collection of marine organisms before you take anything from the beach.

Chapter 1

Bringing the Sea Inside

Setting Up an Aquarium

Having a classroom fish tank is an excellent way to add to your study of marine science. It gives students the ability to observe marine (or fresh water) fish up close. Once set up, an aquarium can be easily maintained for many years. The students can continue their observations and care of the aquarium long after the ocean unit is completed.

Salt Water or Fresh Water

The first decision to make before setting up an aquarium is whether to use fresh water or salt water. Both fresh water aquariums and salt water aquariums have their benefits. In general, fresh water aquariums are easier and cheaper to set up and maintain, while salt water aquariums allow for more exotic, colorful fish. For a classroom aquarium that will not take much time to maintain and that will allow for student participation, a fresh water aquarium is recommended. The following are instructions for setting up a fresh water aquarium. If you wish to set up a salt water aquarium consider investing in a book that will take you through the set-up step by step (like *The Marine Aquarium Reference,* see page 4).

How To Set Up an Aquarium

What Kind of Tank?

The first part of an aquarium system is the tank. When looking for a tank the two things to keep in mind are size and material. You can purchase tanks ranging in size from half-gallon to over 100 gallons, though a rectangular tank between 5 and 20 gallons works best for classroom use. Tanks are made either out of glass or Plexiglas. A glass tank is often less expensive and easier to maintain, while a Plexiglas tank allows for better initial viewing (Plexiglas is easily scratched, and the clarity

of the tank may diminish over time). Whichever tank you purchase, make sure it has a well-fitting lid in order to slow the process of evaporation.

Filter system and other materials

The next piece of equipment you need is a filter system. For short term use an under-gravel filter with an external air pump works well. For any long term use or for a salt water aquarium, an external filter-pump system such as an *Aquaclear* or *Magnum* system is recommended. With an under-gravel filter system you will need filter plates, risers, replaceable charcoal filter media cartridges, air tubing, air stones and an air pump. These materials are often sold as a set. External filter-pump systems are self-contained and often come with filter media that can be replaced periodically.

Other materials that you will need are a lid for the tank, lights, gravel, a thermometer and a heater.* It is also a good idea to purchase a fish net, plants and a scrubbing pad for algae (pads for glass tanks are typically dark blue and pads for Plexiglas tanks are usually white).

* *This might not be necessary if you are in a warm climate or plan to have fish that can tolerate cold water.*

Setting up the aquarium

Once you have all the materials, it is time to set up the aquarium.

- Place the aquarium near an electrical outlet so that you can plug in the pump and light.
- Before you add water, set up the tank, filter and gravel. If you are using an external filter-pump system, all you have to do is mount it on the side of your tank and plug it in to begin use (never plug in a filter-pump system before adding water to the pump.)
- The gravel can then be added to the bottom of the tank. It is always good to wash the gravel before adding water to eliminate any dirt or dust from your tank.
- If you are using an under-gravel filter system, lay the filter plates on the bottom of the tank and then add the risers (plastic cylinders) into each corner. Add the gravel on top of the filter plates once the risers are in place.
- Attach an air stone to the end of a piece of air tubing and insert it into the riser, placing the top containing the filter cartridge on top. If you wish to use two air stones, one in each corner, you will need to connect the two pieces of tubing with a T-shaped connector. From this connector you can run another length of tubing to your external air pump.

Adding water

Now you are ready to add water to your tank. For a fresh water tank, it is best to use filtered water since regular tap water will cause mineral deposits and algae growth. With any type of water you need to use a water conditioner to eliminate chlorine. Water conditioners can be purchased at any pet store that carries fish.

Salt water can be made by adding sea salt to filtered water. Sea salt is different from the salt used for cooking and can also be purchased from a pet store. One brand is *Instant Ocean*. If you live near the ocean, you can also simply collect water from the ocean, but make sure you are collecting from a non-contaminated area. Normal sea water has 34 parts per thousand salt, or 4 tablespoons per gallon.

The best way to get your aquarium ready for fish is to add cup of water from an existing aquarium and allow it to run through the filters for a few days in order to establish a healthy bacteria level. If you do not have access to any other aquariums from which you can borrow water, you will want to make sure that the first fish you add to the aquarium are very hearty. You can also increase the fishes' chance of survival by adding the water your fish came in from the fish store to your tank.

Selecting Fish

Now you are ready to add fish to your aquarium. When choosing fish, make sure that they are compatible. If you get an aggressive chiclid  and a peaceful platy, you will be observing predation firsthand in the classroom. Most good pet stores will be able to tell you which fish are compatible. Often it is good to get several of the same small fish so that they can form schools. The general rule for the number of fish in a tank is one fish per gallon for small fish and one fish per two gallons if they are medium to large fish. It is always best to have too few fish and allow them to have lots of room to swim than to have too many fish that are crowded.

Many people have bought fish and brought them home only to have them die in their tank within a few days. If this happens, take the fish and a sample of water back to the store. Most pet stores will refund your money or give you a new fish. They will also check your water to make sure nothing is wrong in your tank.

Caring for the Aquarium

You will need to feed your fish two to three times a week. When you select the fish at the store, also select a fish food. Most fish will eat flake food, though more exotic fish need special diets. You should only feed the fish as much as they will consume in a few minutes. Extra food will fall to the bottom and cause excess algae growth. You can also purchase feeder tablets that will allow a small amount of food to be released over time. These are good for short vacations when you will not be in the classroom.

One problem that occurs in many tanks is algae growth. The best way to take care of algae growth is to get aquatic snails from the fish store to live in your tank. Not only do they keep the  tank clean, but also they often reproduce by laying small egg packets on the side of the tank. Students can watch the snails eggs grow and hatch if they are removed from the tank (inside the tank the fish often eat them).

If you do not want to use snails, the tank will need to be cleaned with an algae pad every week or two.

You will also need to change the filter medium every three to six months. Partial water changes (taking out a few gallons and replacing them with clean water) are also needed every month. Make sure that every time you add new water, you also add water conditioner. If you want to keep extra care of your tank, you can also check the pH level of the water. Kits containing pH strips are available at fish stores. These can be used simply by putting a drop of water on the strip. The pH of your fish tank should be between 6.8 and 7.2.

How Students Can Participate

Students can participate in setting up the aquarium and caring for the fish. Groups of students can share the responsibility of feeding the fish, cleaning the tank, checking the pH, and changing the water (a partial water change should be done every two to four weeks).

Ecosystems
A Look Into the Tide Pool

Background Information

Ecosystems, Environments and Habitats

Ecology is the scientific study of the relationships among organisms in the same environment. It involves all aspects of the organisms' environment, both living and non-living. An **environment** is the external surroundings of an organism, while an **ecosystem** is a term used to describe an environmental unit that consists of living and non-living parts, interacting to form a stable system. While an ecosystem consists of many animals and plants living together in the same environment, a **habitat** is the living place (home) of one specific organism, characterized by its physical and biological properties.

So if we were to say that an owl lives in a tree, that is its habitat. If we were to describe the tree in terms of its physical properties, the temperature, height of tree, type of tree, soil type, etc., we would be describing the owl's environment. And if we were to describe all the other creatures that live in and around the tree, as well as the physical environment such as temperature, wind, light, soil, and how these interact, we would be describing an ecosystem.

The Tide Pool

The ecosystem that this book will focus on is the tide pool. While you will find that not all activities are focused on the tide pool, it is a theme that runs throughout the book. You can use this as the focus of your unit on the ocean or as just one part of a unit on the entire ocean.

A **tide pool** is found on the seashore where outcroppings of rocks form pools where seawater collects. During the day the level of the water rises and falls due to the tides. At high tide the tide pool is often completely covered with water, and during low tide, the tide pool is left uncovered. There are two high tides and two low tides every day. The tide pool is often exposed to extremes in environmental conditions. The animals that live in the tide pool are adapted to live in an area that can be either wet or dry, hot or cold, underwater or exposed to the air, calm or pounded by waves. And the animals and plants in the tide pool have to protect themselves from predators that come from the sea or the land. It is a very dynamic area that is filled with intriguing creatures.

Tide Pool Inhabitants

Most of the organisms that live in a tide pool are small in comparison to a shark or a whale. There are many small fish such as tide pool **sculpin** that inhabit tide pools, as well as many **baby fish**. In fact, tide pools are often nursery areas for fish, since they are small, protected areas. The tide pool gives baby fish a place to hide while they grow strong before they enter the larger ocean realm.

There are also many invertebrates, or animals without backbones, that live in the tide pools. You can find **sea stars, snails, sea urchins, sponges, hermit crabs, rock crabs, worms, mussels, periwinkles, barnacles, sea anemones, octopus, crabs, shrimp,** and many other animals in tide pools.

Since many of the animals that live in tide pools are invertebrates, you may want to refer to the section on invertebrates (pages 53 to 63). In this section you will find information and pictures of many of the animals referred to above. Information about these tide pool animals can be found as follows:

- sea star - 53
- sea urchin - 54
- sea snail - 55
- crab - 56
- hermit crab - 57
- sea hare - 58
- barnacle - 60
- sea anemone - 61
- limpet - 62

In addition to these invertebrates, you may want to provide your class information about sponges, tide pool sculpins, brittle stars, nudibranches, sea slugs, sea hares, chitons, limpets and coral.

Tide Pool Plants

In addition to animals, a variety of plants can be found in tide pools. **Algae, surf grass,** and **seaweed** are common in tide pools. These plants give small animals a place to hide, as well as something to eat. Like the animals that live in tide pools, they must be specially adapted to survive in this harsh, changing environment.

Chapter Contents

The main concept presented in this chapter is that animals live in different environments. The tide pool is one marine environment. It is a harsh environment and the animals that live in the tide pool are specially adapted to live here. The concepts presented in each lesson are:

2.1 - An introduction to the concepts of organisms, environments and ecosystems

2.2 - An introduction of tide pools as an environment

2.3 - Visual depiction of a tide pool

2.4 - Demonstration of how shells protect sea snails and other shell fish

2.5 - Review of organisms that live in tide pools

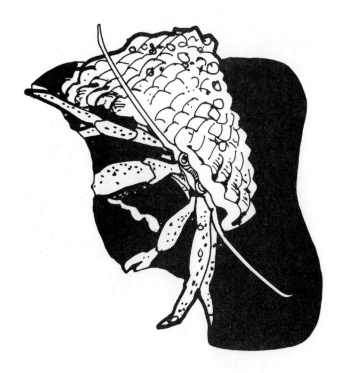

Ecosystems
Activities

Some students will be able to complete the following activities best when thinking of environments and ecosystems that are familiar to them. Other students will be able to build the concepts of ecosystems around environments that may not be as familiar to them, such as the tide pool. These activities can be performed at either of these conceptual levels or by moving from familiar to foreign.

2.1 From Organism to Ecosystem

Overview
This lesson uses drawing to take students from a familiar concept (an organism they already know) to new concepts (environment and ecosystem). The students can do this activity independently, in cooperative groups, or as a class.

Materials
- ✓ paper
- ✓ crayons or colored pencils
  or
- ✓ board space and pens

Procedure
1. Start by having the students draw an animal that they are familiar with. This will be their organism for the rest of this activity. Have them label this drawing **organism**.

2. Next have students make another drawing of where the animal lives. They can include water, air, trees, rocks and other physical objects, but no other animals. Have them label this drawing **environment**.

3. Finally have students make a third drawing in which they show their organism in its environment and include other animals in the environment. They can label this drawing **ecosystem**.

4. Combine the series of drawings in a flip book or display them on a bulletin board.

2.2 Environment Mind Map

Overview
Students will expand their understanding of an environment by naming, drawing or writing the names of animals and plants that live in an chosen environment. The students can do this activity independently, in cooperative groups, or as a class.

Materials
- ✓ paper
- ✓ pencils
  or
- ✓ board space and pens

Procedure
1. As a group, choose an environment, such as a lake, meadow, forest, mountain, river, or sandy beach. Write the name of the environment or draw a simple picture of the environment and then draw a circle around the word or drawing.

2. Have students name as many animals and plants as they can think of that live in that environment. These should be connected with straight lines to the word in the center.

3. Introduce tide pools. Describe what they are (see Background Information). Discuss in general what kind of plants and animals might live in a tide pool (small, tough, able to cling to the rocks, able to be in water or in the air, etc.).

4. Have students make a mind map of a tide pool. See below for a beginning of a mind map for a tide pool.

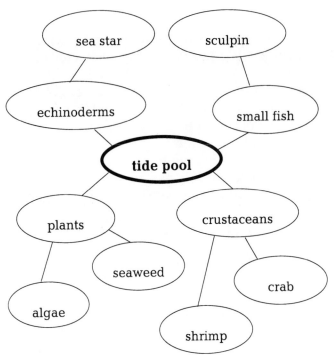

2.3 Build a Tide Pool

Overview
This is an on-going project. This art project gives students an opportunity to demonstrate their understanding of the tide pool environment. There are two ways you can handle this project. You can create a tide pool on a bulletin board or you can build a three-dimensional model using a water-proof tub and actual rocks and sand.

Materials
- ✓ construction paper
- ✓ scissors
- ✓ pens or crayons
- ✓ assorted craft materials

Procedure
1. Using a wall or bulletin board make a drawing that shows air, rocks and ocean. Make sure that your environment shows rocks that make the tide pools and that it shows these pools filled with water (see page 15 for an illustration).

As an alternative, get a shallow tub and place rocks around the edge of the tub. Fill the interior of the tub with rocks and sand. Discuss the fact that in real life, this pool would be filled with only a small amount of water during low tide and completely covered with water during high tide. Since you will be displaying tide pool plants and animals that will be made of paper or clay, do not fill your mock tide pool with water.

2. As your studies progress, create and add organisms such as sea stars, octopus and seaweed to your tide pool. In the end you will have an area teeming with life.

2.4 Why Does a Snail Have a Shell?

Overview
This experiment is meant to demonstrate one reason that sea snails have a shell.

Materials
- ✓ two sponges
- ✓ water
- ✓ one pie plate or other device to cover one sponge

Procedure
1. After you have discussed with your students how sometimes the animals in tide pools are stranded out of the water for several hours, ask them what they think would happen to an ocean animal if it were in the sun for a period of time. Discuss student's ideas, leading them to the conclusion that the animal might get dried out.

2. Get both sponges wet with water. Place both sponges outside under the sun. You will need to make sure it is not raining.

3. Place the pie plate over one of the sponges to represent the shell of a sea snail.

4. Leave the sponges out for an hour or two and check their progress. Have the students find which one dried out first.

5. Ask the students why they think the sponge that was covered did not get as dry. Discuss how the shell on sea snails performs the same function as the pie plate on the sponge, preventing it from getting dried out.

2.5 Tide Pool Treasures

Overview
This lesson tests students recall of organisms you have studied in the previous lessons.

Materials
✓ "Tide Pool Treasures" worksheet
✓ pencils or crayons

Procedure
1. Review some of the tide pool organisms you have studied. Depending on grade level and students' abilities, you will have introduced and studied different numbers and different kinds of organisms.

2. Using your tide pool bulletin board, have students identify the various organisms that are displayed.

3. Have each student draw or write the names of as many tide pool organisms as they can remember on the worksheet entitled "Tide Pool Treasures."

4. Discuss why these plants and animals are well-suited for living in the harsh and changing environment of the tide pool.

If You Live By the Ocean

If you live by the ocean you may have the opportunity to visit a tide pool firsthand. Before you go, make sure to pick a location that allows safe entry into the tide pool area as not all tide pools are easily accessible or safe for young children. Also make sure to check your local tide charts to pick a time when the tide is low. If you go at high tide, the students will not be able to approach the tide pool at all. It is best for students to always wear shoes in tide pools.

Make sure to tell students that all the creatures are alive and that they must be very careful about handling and walking around these fragile creatures. If an animal is attached to a rock, tearing it off will often kill it, so it is best to gently touch animals where they are. Also be aware that in most states it is illegal to take any animals from the tide pool without the proper permits (these are different from fishing permits). If you have a collecting permit and have a salt water aquarium in the classroom, you can collect animals to bring back for observation.

Follow-Up Questions
- What physical stresses do animals that live in a tide pool have to deal with that another ocean or land animal might not?
- What are some adaptations tide pool animals have that allow them to live in such a dynamic environment?
- If you were a tide pool animal, which one would you want to be? Why? Tell what special features enable you to live in a tide pool.
- How is a tide pool like a river? How is it different?
- If you were a small fish, would it be harder to live in the ocean or in a tide pool? Why?

A Tide Pool

15

Tide Pool Treasures

Name _____

Write the names of all the tide pool animals you can think of on the rocks of this tide pool.

What is Seawater?

A Basic Lesson in Chemistry

Background Information
Water, Water Everywhere

The earth is virtually covered in water. Nearly ¾ of the earth's surface is covered in water, 97% of this water lying in the oceans. Without this water, our world would most likely resemble our nearest neighbor, Mars, a dry, lifeless planet. The concept of sea water and how it differs from fresh water can be hard to grasp if you have never been to the ocean, as many people have not. Through these activities students will learn about sea water and some of its properties.

Sea Water

Sea water is approximately 3.4% or 34 parts per thousand (ppt) salt. This means that for every thousand molecules of water, there are 34 molecules of salt. The salinity, or how much salt is in the water, of sea water is very consistent throughout the world's oceans. The highest ocean salinity is found in the Red Sea where it reaches 39 ppt, and the lowest is at the North Pole where it is as low as 32 ppt. This range is quite small in comparison to many lakes and rivers, which can vary from near 0 ppt to over 40 ppt in some isolated lakes. The reason that the salinity of the world's oceans is nearly the same is because of the constant movement of water between oceans by global ocean currents.

But why is the ocean salty? As the forces of erosion break down rocks and minerals from land, small pieces of these minerals, including salt, are carried into the ocean. There are many other minerals dissolved in the ocean water, but salt is the most common, making up over 90% of all dissolved ions in the ocean.

Chapter Contents

The main focus of this chapter is the differences between sea water and fresh water. The specific concepts presented in each lesson are:

3.1 - Assess prior knowledge

3.2 - Demonstrate the proportion of water to land on earth

3.3 - Show how salty water has solid salt suspended in it

3.4 - Demonstrate the effect of salt water on fresh water plants and fresh water on salt water plants

3.5 - Comparison of fresh water and salt water

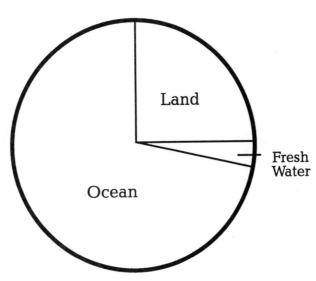

What is Sea Water?

Activities

The best way for young children to recognize the differences between two substances is for them to explore the substances on several levels. All of these activities will use both fresh water and water with salt added to it. The salt water does not have to be the same salinity as the ocean.

3.1 Make a List

Overview
This lesson lets you assess what students already know about the ocean and sea water.

Materials
- ✓ chalk and chalkboard
- ✓ pen and whiteboard
  or
- ✓ pens and paper

Procedure
1. Find out what your class already knows about sea water. Either list on the board or have the students make their own lists of what they know about the ocean and sea water. This could include animals that live in the ocean and how sea water is different from fresh water.

2. If the students are doing this independently, make a class list by compiling all the students' lists.

3. Keep your class list in a visible spot so you can add to it as new concepts are presented.

3.2 Graphing the Earth

Overview
This lesson helps students visualize how much of the earth is covered with water.

Materials
- ✓ "Graphing the Earth" worksheet
- ✓ colored pencils or crayons
- ✓ four glass containers

Procedure
1. Ask students if they think the earth is covered more with land or water. Discuss their perceptions.

2. Show them four glass containers of the same size, three filled with water and one filled with dirt. Tell them that this is the proportion of land and water.

3. Hand out a copy of the worksheet on page 21 to each student along with colored pencils, crayons, or pens.

4. Explain that the circle represents the surface of the earth. It has been divided into three sections representing how much of the earth's surface is covered by land, fresh water (lakes and rivers) and salt water (ocean).

5. Have the students color the land section brown, the fresh water section blue and the salt water section green.

3.3 Evaporation

Overview
This experiment lets students see the salt in salt water.

Materials
- ✓ several foil pie tins or other open containers
- ✓ salt
- ✓ measuring spoon

Procedure
1. Divide students into three groups and distribute three pie tins to each group of students.

2. Have ready one container of fresh water and two containers of salt water of different salinity, each appropriately labeled. For the first container of salt water, mix one teaspoon of salt to every two cups of water. For the second container of salt water mix one teaspoon of salt with every cup of water. Pour a small amount of each kind of water into each group's tins.

3. Let students dip their fingers into each of the dishes of water one at a time and tell you what they taste. Ask them to put their dishes in order from most salty to least salty.

4. Set the tins outside, in a sunny window, or put them over a hotplate.

5. Wait for the water to evaporate and look at what is left in the pie tins. The salt water should leave behind a thin layer of salt. Let the students touch the salt and taste it.

6. Ask them why they think the salt was left behind. Ask them which tin has more salt (the pan that started with the saltiest water).

3.4 Fresh Versus Salt

Overview
This experiment shows the effects of salt water on plants.

Materials
- ✓ water
- ✓ salt
- ✓ measuring spoons
- ✓ two small potted plants
- ✓ two marine plants (from pet store or ocean)
- ✓ containers for fresh and salt water
- ✓ "Fresh or Salty" worksheet

Procedure
1. Prepare a container of fresh water and salt water (1 teaspoon salt per cup of water) and label each. Cover the containers to minimize evaporation.

2. Put the plants where the students can watch them for a week. Label one of the land plants and marine plants "Fresh Water" and the other two "Salt Water." Also number each plant with the numbers one through four.

3. For five days (or longer if you wish) you will give the plants only the type of water that is indicated on their labels.

4. The students will plot their progress by drawing what the plants look like on each day.

5. If you wish to continue the experiment, return all plants to their natural water after the week is up and watch to see if the ones that were given the "wrong" water recover.

6. Ask the students to explain what happened. Why did some plants not do well? What does that tell you about where they live? Do you think the same thing might happen if we put a fish that lives in fresh water into the ocean or an ocean fish in fresh water?

3.5 Word Box

Overview
This lesson is a review of terminology that students have been exposed to while studying water. This can be used as a review or an assessment tool.

Materials
- ✓ "Water Words" worksheet
- ✓ pencils
- ✓ crayons

Procedure
1. As a group review concepts having to do with sea water by reviewing things you have written on your chart (lesson 3.1).

2. Give each student a copy of the worksheet entitled "Water Words" (page 24).

3. Have the students divide the words from the top of the worksheet into two categories, depending on whether they are associated with fresh water or salt water.

4. Discuss how a fresh water habitat (like a river or lake) might be different from a salt water habitat (ocean or tide pool) – different plants, animals, etc.

If You Live by the Ocean

Collect water from several different locations at your local beach, such as the open ocean, near a river mouth, and inside a tide pool at low tide. Repeat the evaporation experiment and see if there are any differences in the amount of salt in each of these types of water.

Follow-Up Questions/Activities
- What have you learned about sea water? Do you think the same kinds of animals and plants could live in salt water as live in fresh water?
- Have students draw a picture of an animal that they think lives in fresh water and one that they think lives in salt water.
- What do you think happens to fresh, river water when it enters the sea?
- How would a rainstorm affect the animals that live in a tide pool?

Graphing the Earth

Name _____

This graph shows what part of the earth is land and what part is water.
Color the part that says "land" brown.
Color the part that says "ocean" green.
Color the part that says "fresh water" blue.

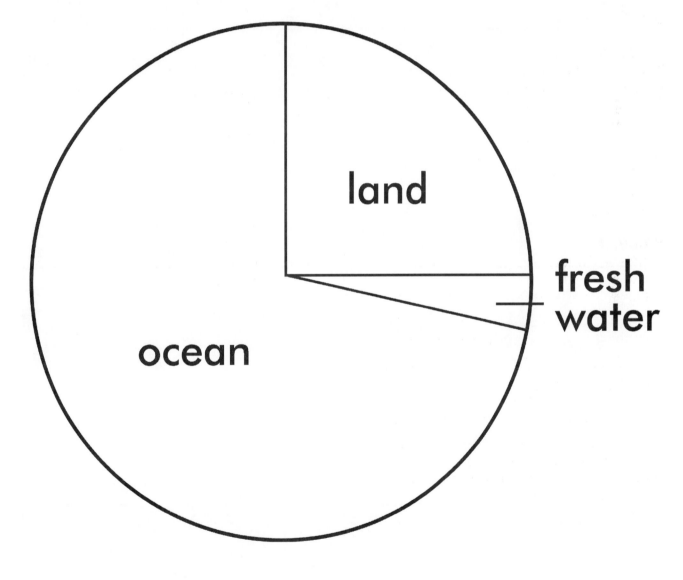

This graph show that _____

_____

Fresh or Salty?

Name _____

Draw pictures to show what the plants look like each day.

Day 1

plant 1	plant 2	plant 3	plant 4

Day 2

plant 1	plant 2	plant 3	plant 4

Day 3

plant 1	plant 2	plant 3	plant 4

Name _____

Day 4

plant 1	plant 2	plant 3	plant 4

Day 5

plant 1	plant 2	plant 3	plant 4

From this experiment I learned_____

_____

_____

_____

_____

_____

_____

_____

Water Words

Name _____

Write each word in the box under either "fresh water" or "salt water."

whale	don't drink	seaweed
drink	ocean	water lily
lake	frog	shark

fresh water   **salt water**

_____   _____

_____   _____

_____   _____

_____   _____

_____   _____

_____   _____

✏️ Add at least two more words or phrases to each list.

✏️ On the back of this paper draw a picture of either a fresh water environment or a salt water environment.

Fish
Animals with Fins and Scales

Background Information

Where Do You Find Fish?

When we think of ocean animals, fish come to mind. You can find fish in almost every body of water in the world, including the ocean, lakes, rivers, streams and estuaries. The thousands of different fish species that inhabit the earth are all built for different lifestyles. They are adapted to live in very cold water found in frozen lakes and at the bottom of the ocean, in fast moving currents near the seashore, or in the complete darkness of caves and at the bottom of ocean trenches. Some are adapted for swimming fast, and others sit quietly on the ocean floor. For almost every type of environment and lifestyle, there is a fish that is well adapted for this type of environment.

Characteristics of Fish

All fish are vertebrates, or animals with backbones. Fish have many bones throughout their bodies, just like humans do. Most fish lay eggs that hatch into tiny fish fry. Sharks are one type of fish. Sharks, unlike many other fish, have bones that are made of soft cartilage, like the material in the outer part of humans' ears.

While there are many similarities between all the different species of fish, there are also many differences. Fish come in many shapes and sizes. They can be long and skinny or shaped like a box. The largest fish is the whale shark, which is almost 18 meters in length; and the smallest fish fry is only a few millimeters long.

All fish have a mouth and nostrils, though they only use their nose to smell, not for breathing. All fish get oxygen from the water through their gills. As water passes through the fish's mouth, it is pushed over the gills that capture the small amounts of oxygen that is in the water.

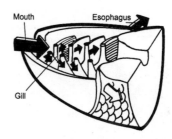

Mouth | Esophagus | Gill

Bony fish have gill covers that protect their gills. Most fish have eyes, though some fish that spend their lives in complete darkness do not. Fish also have scales that cover their body.

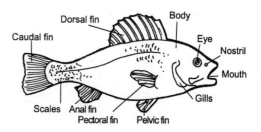

Dorsal fin | Body | Caudal fin | Eye | Nostril | Mouth | Gills | Scales | Anal fin | Pectoral fin | Pelvic fin

Most fish have three sets of major fins – the dorsal fin (on their back), the caudal fin (also known as their tail), and pectoral fins (along their sides). Fish use these fins in different ways, some for steering and others for moving through the water. When it comes to fins, sometimes having none at all helps fish like eels hide in caves. And fast swimming fish like tuna or swordfish need a large deeply forked tail fin to keep them moving. Some fish, like the flying fish, have large pectoral fins that they use for movement, in and out of the water.

Fish eat many different types of food. While some suck up tiny plankton, others munch on algae. Large fish also eat other smaller fish.

Many of the differences that we see in fish are due to their amazing ability to adapt to their environment. A fish's shape, color, mouth, and fins all can help the fish blend in to its habitat or can give it the ability to survive. When we look at body shape, a torpedo-shaped fish is designed for fast movement, a round or disc-shaped fish is designed for small, slow movements, while a flat-bottomed fish is designed for sitting on the sea floor or hard surface.

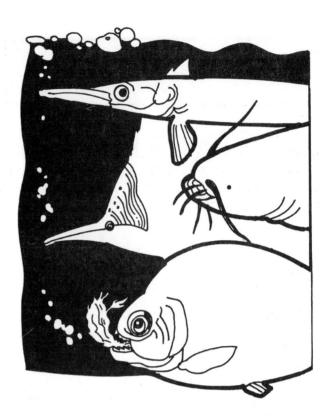

The mouth on a fish can tell you what it eats. Fish that have teeth usually eat other fish or animals, while fish that have their mouth pointing downward or on the underside of their head find their food in the sediment. A long, small mouth helps fish like the butterfly fish find food in cracks and crevices, and the beak-like mouth of the parrot fish helps it scrape algae off rocks. So as you can see, there are a lot of different fish out there, each with their own lifestyle.

The color of a fish can also tell you a lot about its lifestyle. Fish that spend most of their life swimming in the open ocean are dark colored on top and light colored on the bottom. This is called counter shading. Fish that live in colorful places like a coral reef are also brightly colored, and fish that are poisonous (like the lion fish and many box fish) also display their defense in bright color. Many other fish match their color to their surroundings. Some fish like the kelp fish or the flat fish can actually change colors as their environment changes.

Chapter Contents

The main concept in this chapter is that while fish have some common characteristics, there is great variety, and these variations help the fish survive. The concepts presented in the lessons are:

4.1 - Identify the main parts of a fish

4.2 - Match a fish's shape with its ability to swim fast

4.3 - Identify factors that affect a fish's rate of breathing

4.4 - Demonstrate how a fish's coloration allows it to hide from predators

4.5 - Determine what food a fish prefers

Chapter 4

Fish
Activities

The activities in this section will help students learn more about fish. Some of the experiments can be done only if you have set up an aquarium in your classroom or have access to an aquarium in another room. If you have built a model of a tide pool you can have the students create fish to live in the tide pool. Another good activity is to plan a field trip to a local aquarium where the students can view many types of fish.

4.1 Getting to Know a Fish

Overview
In this activity the students will be able to show their knowledge of the parts of the fish. This can be used as a learning tool, a review, or an assessment tool.

Materials
✓ "Getting to Know a Fish" worksheet
✓ pencils

Procedure
1. Make a copy of the worksheet on page 31 for the overhead projector and also give each student a copy of the worksheet.

2. Using the guide below, help students identify the external features of a fish and write the words on their worksheets.

3. Discuss what each body part is used for (see Background Information).

4. For a lasting display, make an enlargement of the fish on a bulletin board and label the external features of the fish.

4.2 Fish Shapes

Overview
In this activity students will look at the shape of a fish and try to determine something about its lifestyle and how quickly it can swim.

Materials
✓ "Fish Shapes" worksheet
✓ pencils

Procedure
1. Begin the exercise by asking the students which moves faster, a rocket or a balloon. Then ask students if they have noticed that fish have different shapes. Talk about what shapes they have seen before and how these shapes are suited for different movement and eating habits.

2. Give each student a copy of the worksheet on page 32.

3. Discuss why the fish are suited for these activities. What kind of body would be good for a fish that:
   - needs to swim fast to catch its food
   - lives in cracks of the rocks
   - eats other medium sized fish
   - hides in sea grass
   - jumps out of the water

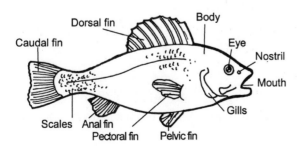

4.3 Fish Breathing

Overview

This experiment is designed for the students to monitor the breathing of a fish without harming the fish. This activity is best done in four small groups. If you have more than one fish in your tank, make sure that all groups use the same type of fish.

Materials

- ✓ fish in an aquarium
- ✓ clock
- ✓ dark cover for tank
- ✓ warm water

Procedure

1. Tell students that fish, like people, need to breathe. Discuss how fish breathe. Ask, "How can you tell if a fish is breathing?"

2. Discuss when people might breathe fast or slow (after running, when asleep, etc.).

3. Have one group of students count how many times the fish opens its mouth in 30 seconds. Every time the fish opens its mouth, it is breathing by taking water over its gills. Record this number on the board.

4. Next, cover the tank with a dark cover for half an hour; this simulates night for the fish. After a half an hour, have the next group of students count the number of times the fish opens its mouth in 30 seconds. Record this number also.

5. Have the third group of students wait at least 15 minutes with the cover off the tank before beginning their trial. Add a few cups of hot (not boiling) water to the tank. The larger the tank, the more hot water you will need to add. All you want to do is raise the temperature of the water a few degrees. Again, have the students count how many breaths the fish takes in 30 seconds.

6. Once the temperature of the tank has returned to normal, have the last group of students count the number of breaths in 30 seconds. See if this count is equal to your first count.

7. Discuss the results of the experiment.

4.4 Camouflage

Overview

This activity lets the students create their own camouflaged fish and a background that it can hide in.

Materials

- ✓ large paper
- ✓ string
- ✓ fish shapes
- ✓ tissue paper
- ✓ paste
- ✓ hole punch
- ✓ tape

Procedure

1. Explain that sometimes animals have to hide from other animals that might want to eat them. Discuss some animals that students are familiar with whose coloring allows them to blend into their environment.

2. Tell students that fish need to blend into their surroundings also. Ask students to suggest what colors and textures a fish should be if it were going to blend in with seaweed, rocks, or the sandy ocean bottom.

3. Give each student one large piece of paper, two lengths of string (over twice the length of the paper), two fish shape cutouts, bright colored tissue paper squares, dull colored tissue paper squares and paste.

4. Have students fold their piece of paper in half, matching the short ends together. Unfold the paper and using a hole punch, punch two holes in each of the short sides of the paper.

5. Then have students paste the dull colored tissue paper on the left side of the paper and the bright colored tissue paper on the right side. Give them fish to cut out (see guide on page 30). Have them also cover one of the fish with bright colored tissue paper and the other with dark colored tissue paper.

6. Now attach a piece of string to each of the fish by taping one piece of string down the length of each fish. Then thread the loose ends of each string through the top or bottom set of holes on the paper and tie the ends together in the back. You will have one fish attached through the top two holes and the other through the bottom two holes. Put the dull colored fish on the dull colored background and the bright colored fish on the bright background. With the string they can "swim" the fish to the opposite side and see why it is good for a fish to be camouflaged.

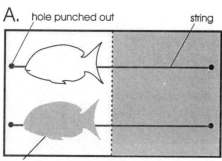

A. hole punched out   string

Tape string to back of fish

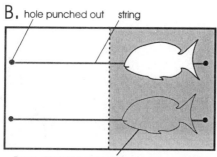

B. hole punched out   string

Tape string to back of fish
pull back and forth to see camouflag effect

7. Show the class color pictures of different fish and discuss how their coloration allows them to blend in with their surroundings.

4.5 Fish Food

Overview
In this activity the students will give fish several different types of food to see which one they prefer. If you have several fish in your aquarium, you might want to keep track of which fish prefers what type of food. It is best to do the trials on separate days so that the fish are always hungry.

Materials
✓ fish in an aquarium
✓ stop watch or clock
✓ several types of food such as lettuce, flake food, shrimp

Procedure
1. Ask students if they have favorite foods. Take a survey to see what food students prefer.

2. Speculate whether fish have a preference in food. Ask, "How do you think we could test which foods the fish in our aquarium like to eat?" Propose feeding the fish different foods and seeing if they eat the food and how quickly they eat it.

3. Start your experiment by giving the fish their normal flake food and record how long it takes to eat all the food. If it is more than 15 minutes, stop timing.

4. The next day try giving the fish another type of food and record how long it takes to eat it all. Again, stop timing if it is more than 15 minutes. If the food is not eaten within a few hours, take it out and give the fish a little of its flake food.

5. Continue this for several days, trying a new food each day. Record your results each day.

6. Talk about what the fish preferred and why the fish "liked" the food. What is it they like about their favorite food?

If You Live By the Ocean

If you live by the ocean you may have the opportunity to visit a tide pool firsthand and look for fish. While many creatures live on the rocks, you will need to find deep depressions in the rocks that hold water in order to find small fish. Many of the fish are small and well-camouflaged, so you will have to look closely. Please read the section on tide pools for more directions on safe tide pooling.

Follow-Up Questions/Activities

- Have students think about how different fish are adapted to their environment. Give them an environment, such as the bright coral reef or dark, deep ocean, and have them design a fish that lives there.

- Show pictures of a fish or shark from books and ask students to try and guess if they are fast or slow swimmers, if they live on the sea floor, or swim around in the water. Ask if there is anything else they can guess about the fish's life by looking at its body.

Guide for fish for lesson 4.4

Getting to Know a Fish

Name _____

Label the parts of a fish by writing the words in the box by the parts of the fish.

mouth	caudal fin	dorsal fin
scales	body	gills
	eye	
	nostril	

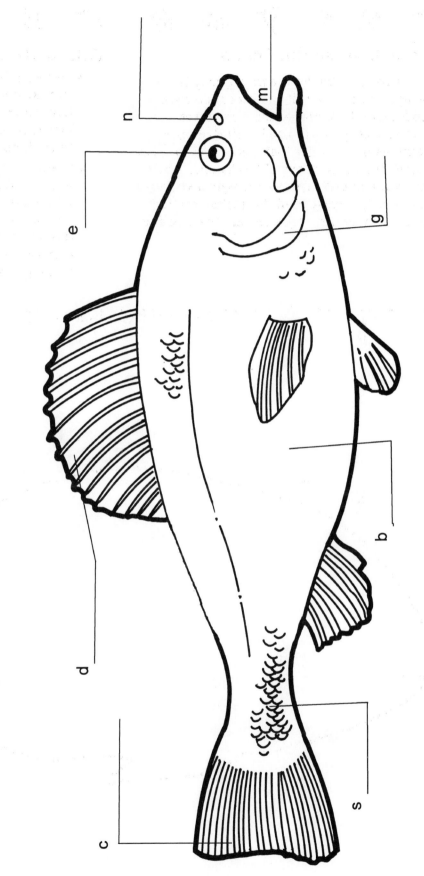

Fish Shapes

Name _____

Draw a ☐ around the fish that can swim fast.

Draw a ◯ around the fish that lives on the sandy ocean bottom.

Draw a △ around the fish that can eat food in cracks.

Marine Mammals
Splashing, Spouting Animals

Background Information
Common Traits

Whales, dolphins, seals, sea lions, sea otters, walruses and polar bears are all marine mammals. Mammals are a group of vertebrates (animals with backbones) that all share common traits. These traits are:

- All mammals are warm blooded.
- Almost all mammals bear live young (the platypus lays eggs).
- All mammals nurse their young.
- All mammals breathe air through their lungs.
- Most mammals have hair (in some marine mammals hair is lost or drastically reduced in adult forms).

There are many types of mammals in the world, and most of them live on land. Other mammals besides marine mammals include cats, dogs, elephants, pigs, cows, monkeys, deer, mice, bears, and humans. What makes marine mammals different from other mammals is that they spend a majority of their lives (if not all of their lives) in the water.

Marine mammals are found in all oceans of the world and in a few rivers. While all marine mammals live in the water, they all must come to the surface to breathe. How long they can hold their breath varies from species to species, though some can hold their breath for as long as two hours, allowing them to dive deep into the ocean. Since all mammals are warm-blooded, they must keep a constant body temperature. Many marine mammals insulate themselves against the cold ocean water by growing a thick layer of blubber, while others use fur.

Variations

Though we often think of all marine mammals as being the same, there is a wide variety among this group. Some, like dolphins, are built for swimming fast and catching fish with their sharp teeth; while others, like manatees, are large and slow moving and prefer to munch on plants or filter their food out of the water. Marine mammals also come in many sizes. The largest animal ever to live on the earth is a blue whale, which is as long as three school buses end to end (100 feet). Other smaller marine mammals are the size of a dog. In the following activities you will have the opportunity to learn more about some of these creatures.

Chapter Contents

This chapter introduces students to marine mammals and gives them an appreciation for how these animals are adapted to live in the ocean. The concepts presented in each lesson are:

5.1 - Basic knowledge of marine mammals

5.2 - External characteristics of a whale

5.3 - How marine mammals compare to humans

5.4 - How baleen compares to teeth

5.5 - How whales and dolphins use echolocation

5.6 - A visual depiction of the size of whales

Marine Mammals
Activities

5.1 Marine Mammal Picture Cards

Materials
- ✓ picture cards, pages 40 - 47
- ✓ crayons
- ✓ staples or hole punch and string
- ✓ cardboard
- ✓ glue

Pages 40 - 47 contain information about specific marine mammals and drawings of the animals. There are several different ways that you can use these cards.

How to Use the Cards
- ■ Use the animal cards to introduce the animals to the class. Have students share what they already know about the animal.
- ■ Enlarge the pictures and put them on a bulletin board. Put a map of the world in the center of the display. Use strings to show where each animal can be found.
- ■ Have students look up the animals in a reference book and color them the correct color.
- ■ Assign each group an animal. Have the students visit the school library to learn more about their group's animal.
- ■ As the students learn about the animals, give them a card to color. At the end of the unit combine all the cards into a book that the students can take home.
- ■ Duplicate four sets of the cards, glue them to cardboard and laminate them. Use the deck of cards to play the card game "Go Fish."
- ■ After your unit on marine mammals, use the cards in an assessment game. Have each student pick one card out of a box and tell you one or two things about the animal.

5.2 Getting to Know a Whale

Overview
In this activity the students will be able to show their knowledge of the parts of the whale. This can be used as a learning tool, a review, or an assessment tool.

Materials
- ✓ "Getting to Know a Whale" worksheet
- ✓ pencils

Procedure
1. Ask students what they already know about whales. Make a list of information they volunteer (providing it is correct information).
2. Discuss the fact that a whale is a mammal. Ask students to name other mammals. List a few mammals. Then discuss what these animals have in common.
3. Tell students that whales have many of the same body parts as other mammals, but they have some unique body parts that other mammals do not have. They have fins and flukes that help them swim in the water.
4. Give each student a copy of the "Getting to Know a Whale" worksheet on page 38 and as a group have them fill in the names of the parts of the whale.

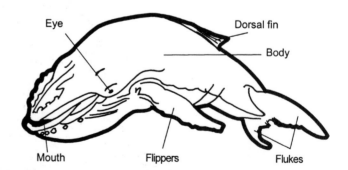

5.3 Marine Mammals and Me

Overview
In this activity students will have the opportunity to compare a marine mammal to themselves. This activity should be done after the attributes of a mammal have been discussed in class. This can be used as a learning tool, a review or an assessment tool.

Materials
- ✓ "Marine Mammals and Me" worksheet
- ✓ pencils

Procedure
1. Review what mammals are and their common attributes.

2. On the board, make a Venn diagram that has two circles. Label one "cows" and one "cats." Fill in the one circle with things that are attributes of cows and one with attributes of cats. In the intersecting section, write some common attributes.

3. Tell students that now they are going to look at two other mammals (humans and seals) and see what things they have in common and how they are different.

4. Give each student a copy of the worksheet entitled "Marine Mammals and Me" and a pencil.

5. Have the students draw a line between the person and its characteristics. Then have them do the same for the seal.

6. Discuss the characteristics that are the same and different for the seal and the person.

5.4 Baleen Versus Teeth

Overview
This simulation will let students see how a whale's baleen enables it to strain food from the water.

Materials
- ✓ tub of water
- ✓ tongs
- ✓ paintbrushes
- ✓ ping-pong balls
- ✓ small pieces of felt, plastic or foam

  The tongs represent teeth or a toothed whale, the paintbrush represents the baleen of a toothless whale, the ping-pong balls represent fish, and the bits of felt, plastic or foam are plankton.

Procedure
1. Tell students that some whales have teeth, but some whales have baleen instead of teeth. Show them a picture of baleen using the marine mammal picture cards and use the information provided to explain what baleen is. Explain that they will do an experiment that shows how these two different types of mouths let whales get their food.

2. Fill a tub or sink with water and put the "fish" and "plankton" in the tub. In small groups, give each student a tool, either tongs or a paintbrush, and tell them about their feeding apparatus. Have the students try to catch the food with the different tools. Have them count how much of each type of food they were able to pick out of the water.

3. As a class, discuss what types of food they think toothed whales and baleen whales eat based on the experiment.

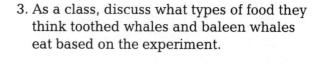

5.5 Echolocation Game

Overview
Echolocation is the ability to navigate using sound waves. This game will illustrate how whales and dolphins use echolocation to find food.

Materials
✓ blindfold
✓ playing area

Procedure
1. Have one student stand up and tell him or her to walk forward as far as he or she can. When the student stops because he or she has approached a wall or another obstacle, ask, "How did you know to stop?"

2. Discuss the fact that people use their eyes to provide information that lets them navigate without running into things. Tell students that dolphins and whales have a different way of "seeing." They use sound waves (sonar) to tell them where objects are so they can move toward them, away from them, or around them. Today they will play a game that will show them how echolocation works.

3. Have students stand in a large circle. Choose one student to be the dolphin. Blindfold her and put her in the center of the circle. Turn the student around a few times.

4. When the blindfolded student stands still she can clap. If she is facing another student, that student will clap back. The blindfolded student must walk slowly towards the sound. She can stop and clap again if she needs to. The student wins the round when she has successfully located another student.

5. Discuss the fact that whales and dolphins do not clap, but they emit sounds that bounce off of objects in the ocean. This helps them locate food and also locate objects so they do not run into them.

5.6 How Big Are Whales?

Overview
Students often want to know how large certain animals are or what the largest animal in a certain group is. This activity will give students the opportunity to really experience how large some whales are.

Materials
✓ yard or meter stick
✓ chalk

Procedure
1. Ask students to tell you about the biggest mammal they have encountered. They will probably describe an elephant that they have seen in a zoo or circus. Explain that whales are very large animals and today they will make some measurements that will show how big these animals are.

2. You will need a large flat area such as a playground to make your whale models. You can choose any of the whales in the following table to use for your activity. Students often are interested in the largest and smallest whale, as well as any that they have seen or studied.

3. Take the students out to the playground. Have one student lie on the ground and measure how tall they are. Draw a line with chalk from their head to their toes showing their height. Next choose a whale. Either measure the appropriate distance using a yardstick or have several students lie down head to toe until you have enough students to measure the length of that whale. Draw a line to show this whale's size.

4. If you are going to measure more than one whale, make sure you label the lines with the names and lengths of the whales.

5. If you wish, you can also have your students draw a picture of the whale that is equal to its size on the playground.

Whale measurements

blue whale – 100 feet – 30 meters
sperm whale – 59 feet – 18 meters
right whale – 57 feet – 17 meters
humpback whale – 50 feet – 15 meters
gray whale – 40 feet – 12 meters
orca (killer whale) – 27 feet – 9 meters
beluga whale – 14 feet – 4.5 meters
bottle nosed dolphin – 12 feet – 4 meters
dwarf sperm whale – 8 feet – 2.4 meters

If You Live by the Ocean

If you live by the ocean you might have the opportunity to see marine mammals in their natural habitat. A field trip on a whale watching boat is an excellent way to see marine mammals of all types first hand. Whale watching is often a seasonal outing so you should check with your local marina to book a trip during the appropriate time of the year. If a whale watching trip is not possible, there are some places where you can see marine mammals such as seals, sea lions and dolphins from shore. Again, inquire where such a location near you may be found that is suitable for students to visit. Be sure to warn students not to approach these marine mammals. All viewing should be done from a safe distance, preferably with binoculars.

Follow-Up Questions/Activities

- Have the students draw a picture of their favorite marine mammal and make up a story about it. They can present these stories orally to the class or write them on paper.
- Why do you think many marine mammals have a thick layer of fat under their skin?
- Make a food chain that includes a marine mammal.
- Make a long list of statements about marine mammals, some of which are facts (many whales migrate to warm waters to give birth) and some of which are opinions (people should not kill cute baby seals). Have students differentiate between facts and opinions.

Getting to Know a Whale

Name _____

Use the words in the box to label the parts of a whale.

eye	mouth	flukes
body	flipper	dorsal fin

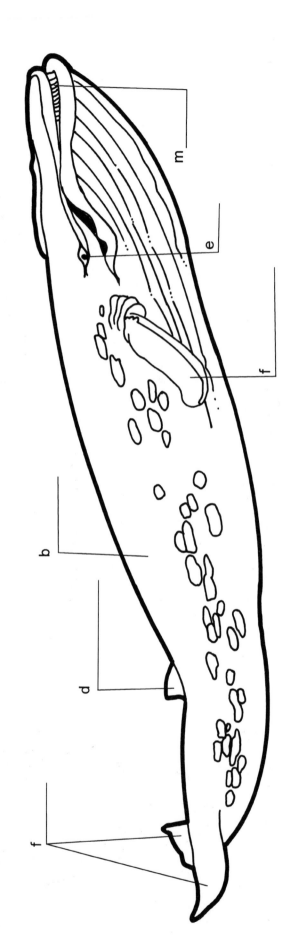

Marine Mammals and Me

Name _____

Draw lines to the person to show which things are true for people. Draw lines to the seal to show which things are true for seals. Some statements are true for both people and seals.

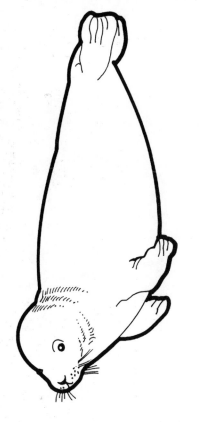

has hair

breaths air

lives on land

lives in the ocean

baby drinks milk

has hands

fast swimmer

eats fish

has bones

has a warm body

© Dandy Lion - *Marine Science, 1*

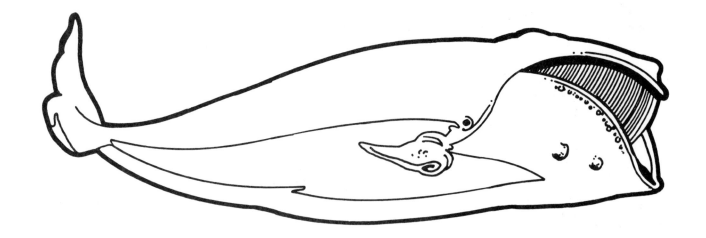

Baleen Whale

Baleen whales are the largest animals to ever live on earth. They include the blue whale, gray whale, humpback whale, and many others. They can be found in all the oceans of the world. Since they are large, they move very slowly. They spend most of their time alone.

Instead of teeth, they have long sheets of baleen that hang from the top of their mouths. Baleen is made of a material like our fingernails. It looks like large paint brushes. It ranges in size from 1 foot to 8 feet long. Whales use the baleen to filter small shrimp called krill and other small creatures out of the water.

Many baleen whales make long migrations between summer feeding areas in cold water and winter breeding areas in warm water. They give birth to their babies in warm water. They have a thick layer of blubber to keep them warm.

On the top of their heads they have a blowhole with two openings that they use to get air. They come to the surface to get air then hold their breaths for a long time when they are under water. The "spout" that you can see when they come to the surface is not water, but warm air from their lungs.

Toothed Whale

Toothed whales such as the orca (killer whale) are smaller, fast-swimming whales. Other toothed whales are the sperm whale, narwhale, and beluga whale. Toothed whales can be found in all oceans of the world, but especially in cold-water areas. Unlike the baleen whales, toothed whales have a mouth full of cone-shaped teeth. They use their swimming abilities to hunt and catch prey such as fish.

They are social animals that form groups or pods. They often hunt in packs and use their large numbers to attack larger whales and sharks. They also eat seals, dolphins, sea otters, squid and walrus. They use their good eyesight and echolocation to find food. Whales and dolphins use echolocation by sending out clicks of sound that bounce off other objects and reflect back to them, like the sound of an echo.

On the top of their heads they have a blowhole that they use to get air. Their blowholes have only one opening. They come to the surface to get air but can then hold their breaths for a long time when they are under water. Many of the toothed whales have pronounced dorsal fins.

Dolphins and Porpoises

Dolphins and porpoises are types of toothed whales. The differences between the two are that the dolphin has an elongated nose (or rostrum) and the porpoise has a rounded nose. Dolphins also have a curved dorsal fin, while porpoises have a triangular dorsal fin.

Like other toothed whales, they are fast swimmers and use their teeth to catch fish and squid. They are also social animals and often are found in large groups. Dolphins and porpoises live in the temperate and tropical oceans of the world as well as some rivers in South America and Asia. Like the other toothed whales, they have good eyesight and echolocation.

Dolphins are larger than porpoises. They are the fastest swimmers and most playful of all the whales. They are intelligent and can learn to do difficult tricks. Dolphins talk to each other using sounds like squeals and clicks. While they have good eyesight, they make sounds and listen for the echoes to help them locate things they cannot see.

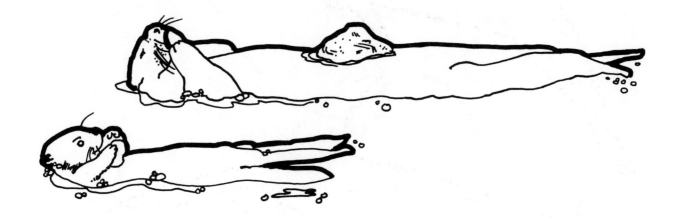

Sea Otter

Sea otters are small marine mammals that live in the kelp forests off the coasts of Japan, Alaska, Canada, Washington, Oregon and California. They have sleek, furry bodies, long tails and short legs with webbed feet. Instead of having a layer of blubber, they are covered by a thick coat of fur. They have sharp teeth and eat fish and hard shelled animals like sea urchins, abalone, crabs and clams that they find while swimming near the rocky floor of the kelp forest.

Sea otters spend much of their time on top of the water wrapped in kelp to keep them from floating away or from being attacked by a passing shark or killer whale. In order to break open the hard shells of its food, a sea otter will float on its back and use a flat rock placed on its belly as a tool to break the shells against.

At one time sea otters were hunted for their fur and almost became extinct. Now you can find a lot of them swimming and diving near the shore.

Seals and Sea Lions

Seals and sea lions are coastal marine mammals that live in the water but also spend a lot of their time resting on land or ice sheets. They are social animals. When they are out of the water, they can be found in groups of over 1,000 individuals. They can be found in all oceans of the world.

There are a couple of differences between seals and sea lions. Sea lions have ear flaps, can bend their rear flippers under their body, can sit upright, and can use their long front flippers to swim.

Seals mainly use their strong rear flippers for swimming. They are good swimmers, but they are awkward and move with difficulty when on land. The males are much larger than the females.

Both seals and sea lions have sharp teeth that they use to eat fish, squid, octopus and shellfish. Their main enemies are sharks, killer whales and polar bears. While all seals and sea lions have coats of fur, they also have a layer of blubber to keep them warm and help them float.

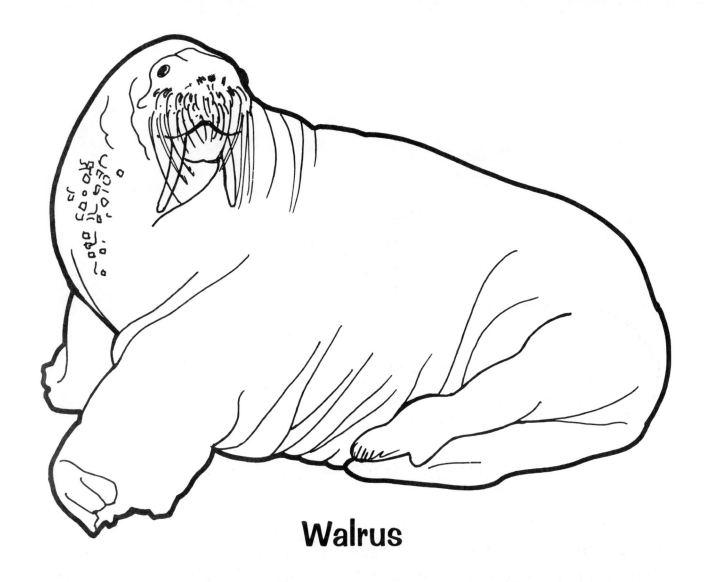

Walrus

The walrus lives in the chilly waters of the Arctic. The walrus is related to seals and sea lions, but it looks very different. Walruses have two large tusks or teeth that grow out of their upper jaws. With these two large tusks the walrus pulls its large body up on sheets of ice.

While the walrus is a marine mammal, it spends a lot of time out of water sleeping on ice or rocks. The walrus uses its whiskers to find clams, crabs, snails and worms in the muddy bottom of the ocean. Like seals and sea lions, the walrus has both a coat of fur and blubber to keep itself warm. It has a bark that sounds like a dog's bark. Some types of walruses are nearly extinct.

Manatee

Manatees are endangered marine mammals that live in the shallow coastal waters of Florida, the Gulf of Mexico, the Caribbean Sea, coastal South America, and west Africa. They are often found in shallow bays, coastal rivers and reefs.

Manatees are the only marine mammals that are plant eaters. A manatee can eat as much as 100 pounds of underwater plants a day. An adult manatee can be up to 12 feet long and weigh 3,000 pounds.

Since manatees are large slow-moving animals that float near the surface of the water, they are often injured by pollution that runs off the land and also by being hit by fast-moving boats.

Unlike other marine mammals, manatees have a tail that is a round paddle. Like the walrus, they have whiskers around their mouths that they use for feeling the ocean floor.

46

Polar Bear

Polar bears are not often thought of as marine mammals, but since they spend much of their time in the cold waters of the Arctic looking for food, they are in fact marine mammals. Polar bears are the only bears that are white in color to blend in with their icy surroundings. Even though the polar bear looks white, its skin is black so that it can absorb heat from the sun to keep itself warm.

They spend most of their time alone, except for cubs that stay close to their mothers. Polar bears are fairly good swimmers and have been seen swimming 50 miles away from ice or land. Polar bears eat fish and seals. They dive beneath ice sheets to look for their food. They can also walk long distances across ice in order to find food.

Chapter 6 — Animals Without Backbones
Squishy, Slippery Animals

Background Information

What are Invertebrates?

Most of the animals on earth are invertebrates (animals without backbones). They include animals such as jellyfish, coral, mussels sponges, worms, crabs, clams, snails, sea stars, octopuses, limpets, sea hares, sea anemones, flatworms, tube worms, sea slugs, barnacles, sea urchins, sand dollars, ladybugs, grasshoppers, ants and spiders. Both in the number of individual animals and in the number of different species, invertebrates far outnumber vertebrates (animals with backbones), especially in the ocean.

Invertebrates are found in all environments from deep-sea trenches to dry deserts. Invertebrates are the predominant life form in the tide pool environment. They can fly through the air or swim in the ocean. They can be as tiny as a speck of dust or as large as a bus. Some are fast swimmers and others spend their entire life in one place. Some have thick, hard shells, while others are very fragile.

Shells and No Shells

Since invertebrates do not have bones like vertebrates, some of them use hard external "shells" or exoskeletons for protection. Animals like snails, mussels, and clams have one or two hard shells that are attached to their bodies and grow as they grow. Other animals like crabs, spiders, dragonflies, and shrimp have a hard outside skeleton that is like a suit of armor that does not grow but is discarded about once a year and replaced with a larger shell. Many invertebrates (squid, jellyfish, and worms), however, have soft bodies. These animals use other means such as camouflage, poison, teeth or fast movement for protection.

Some invertebrates, such as sponges, are very simple animals, with no organs, nervous system or eyes. Others, like the octopus, are very complex and have well-developed organ and nervous systems and are quite intelligent.

Chapter Contents

The aim of this chapter is to present some of the most common marine invertebrates and to acquaint students with some of their special features. The concepts presented in each lesson are:

6.1 - Basic knowledge of invertebrates

6.2 - How invertebrates compare to humans

6.3 - How invertebrates compare to vertebrates

6.4 - Classification of shells

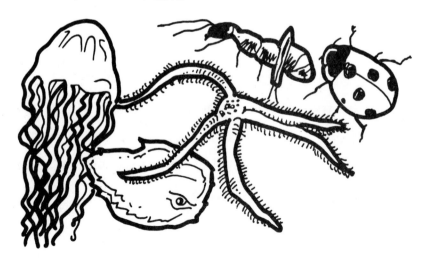

Animals Without Backbones

Activities

6.1 Invertebrate Picture Cards

Materials
- ✓ picture cards
- ✓ crayons
- ✓ staples or hole punch and string
- ✓ cardboard
- ✓ glue

Pages 53 to 63 contain information about specific marine invertebrate animals and drawings of the animals. There are several different ways that you can use these cards.

Ways to Use the Cards
- Use the picture cards to introduce the animals to the class. Have students share what they already know about the animals.
- Cut out the pictures, color them and add them to the tide pool mural you started earlier in this unit. See page 13 for instructions.
- Have students look up the animals in a reference book and then color them the correct color.
- Copy and cut apart these cards and distribute them to groups of students. These animals can become the groups' "mascots." Have students visit the school library to learn more about their group's animal.
- As the students learn about the animals, give them a card to color. At the end of the unit combine all the cards into a book that the students can take home.
- Duplicate four sets of the cards, glue them to cardboard, and laminate them. Use the cards to play "Go Fish." Students must get an entire set of four pictures of the same animal before they can lay down their set of cards.

6.2 Invertebrates and Me

Overview
In this activity students will have the opportunity to compare an invertebrate to themselves. This activity should be done after the attributes of an invertebrate have been discussed in class.

Materials
- ✓ "Invertebrates and Me" worksheet
- ✓ pencils

Procedure
1. Have students bend over and as they roll up, feel their spines. Discuss how bones keep us erect and allow us to move. Introduce the concept of invertebrates (animals without backbones). Ask if they know of some animals that don't have backbones. Make a list.

2. Show pictures of some marine invertebrates and then give each student a copy of the worksheet "Invertebrates and Me."

3. Have the students draw lines between the person and its characteristics. Then have them do the same for the octopus.

4. Discuss the characteristics that are the same and different for the octopus and the person.

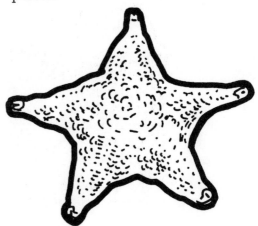

6.3 Vertebrates Versus Invertebrates

Overview
This activity will help students categorize several different animals depending on whether they are invertebrates or vertebrates.

Materials
- ✓ "Backbones or No Backbones" worksheet
- ✓ pencils

Procedure
1. Ask students to name some animals that live on the land that have backbones and also some without backbones (slugs, worms, various insects). Then have them do the same with animals that live in the water.

2. Hand out copies of the worksheet and have students mark the vertebrate and invertebrate animals appropriately.

3. Discuss what adaptations animals have that make up for not having a backbone.

6.4 Sorting Shells

Overview
In this activity groups of students will sort shells by common features. You can get shells from a hobby store or you can order them from a biological supply source.

Materials
- ✓ shells of many sizes, shapes and colors

Procedure
1. Explain that some marine mammals that do not have backbones do have hard shells. Ask why an animal would need a shell.

2. Divide students into groups and give each group of students a collection of shells.

Have them sort them by size, color, shape or whether they are singular shells or composed to two shells joined together (bivalve). Once all the shells are sorted have them explain why they choose to sort them the way they did.

3. Explain that this procedure is much the same as the way scientists sort animals into groups with similar characteristics.

If You Live by the Ocean

If you live by the ocean, visit a tide pool firsthand and look for marine invertebrates. This is an ideal location for observing them. You can find snails, sea stars, limpets, crabs, sea anemones, and maybe even an octopus. Many of the invertebrates are small and well-camouflaged, so you will have to look closely. Lift up seaweed or rocks carefully to look for hidden animals. But be careful where you walk, as many invertebrates will be right underfoot. Please read the section on tide pools for more directions on safe tide pooling.

Follow-Up Questions/Activities
- How are invertebrates like vertebrates? How are they different?
- What special features do invertebrates have that allow them to survive without a backbone?
- Have the students draw a picture of their favorite invertebrate tide pool animal and tell how it is adapted to survive in the tide pool.
- Have the class list some things that might be difficult about not having a backbone and how some of the animals deal with these problems.

Invertebrates and Me

Name _____

Draw lines to show what things describe the person and what things describe the octopus.

has eyes

has bones

has a soft body

lives in the water

lives on land

has hands

has tentacles

has a brain

eats fish

eats apples

has a heart

has suction cups

Backbones or No Backbones?

Name _____

Draw a ◯ around the animals with backbones (vertebrates).

Draw an ✖ on the animals without backbones (invertebrates).

Sea Star

The sea star is one of the best known tide pool animals. It gets its name from its five arms, each with rows of tiny tube feet on the underside. These tube feet have lots of powerful suction cups on the ends and help the sea star hold on to rocks while the waves crash around it.

Sea stars are a group of animals called echinoderms. Echinoderm means "spiny skin." Sea stars have small spines all over their bodies. Other relatives of the sea star are sea urchins, sand dollars and sea cucumbers.

Sea stars can be found in many coastal areas. They are scavengers, eating a variety of different things. The sea star's favorite food is mussels. It pulls the two shells of the mussel apart and sticks its stomach into the shell to eat the mussel.

If a sea star loses an arm, it can regrow it. The sea star has no brain and no true eyes, but it has light-sensitive spots on the end of each arm.

Sea Urchin

The sea urchin is an echinoderm like the sea star. The sea urchin is shaped like a ball, but with thousands of red or purple spines all over its body. The spines are often poisonous.

Like a sea star, it also has tube feet, but the sea urchin's feet are all over the body, not just on the bottom. The sea urchin uses its tube feet to cling onto rocks and algae and to get its food. The sea urchin has a mouth with five teeth on the bottom of its body, just like sea star. It uses its five teeth to scrape algae off the rocks and to bite pieces of algae.

Since the sea urchin has long spines, not many other animals like to eat it. One of its enemies is the large wolf eel.

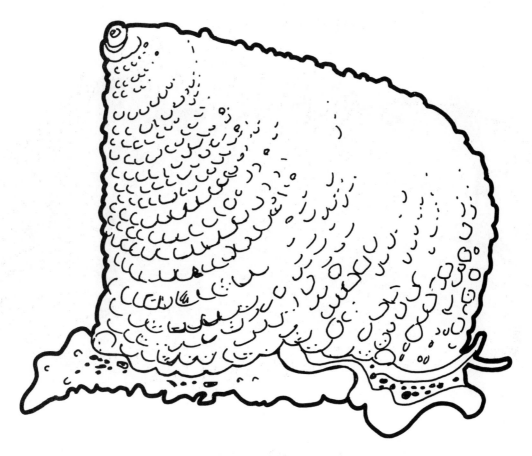

Sea Snail

The sea snail, like garden snails, carries a large shell on its back protecting its soft body. Sea snails come in a variety of sizes and colors. Some are as small as the head of a pin. Others are as large as a softball.

The sea snail is slow-moving and uses its strong foot to keep it from being washed out of the tide pool by strong waves. The shell of the sea snail is very thick and has a trap door called an operculum. The snail can close its trap door if a predator comes near.

The sea snail likes to scrape algae off the rocks in the tide pool for food. It has a rough zipper-like tongue called a radula that is used to eat algae. The sea snail has eyes and a small brain. When the tide is out the sea snail often closes into its shell to keep from drying out in the hot sun.

Sea snails lay hundreds of fry eggs on the rocks. When the baby snails hatch, they drift around in the ocean as plankton until they are large enough to hold onto rocks.

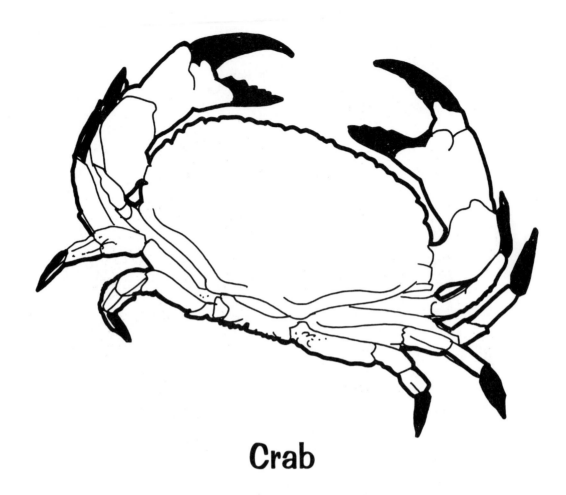

Crab

Crabs are covered with a hard shell called a carapace that forms from a layer of their skin. The shell is like a suit of armor, and it protects the crab from its predators. When the crab grows too big for its shell, it wiggles out and makes a new one. This is called molting.

Crabs have eight jointed legs that they use for walking and two legs that are pinchers. Crabs can run fast, usually either moving sideways or backwards. Crabs have good eyesight and can see everything that is going on around them in the tide pool.

Crabs are crustaceans and are related to other animals such as lobsters, shrimp, barnacles, and insects. Crabs live in many environments. While most live in sea water, some live in fresh water, and some even live on land. They come in a variety of sizes and colors.

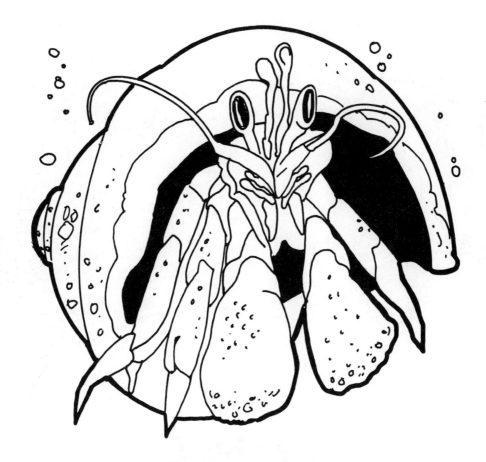

Hermit Crab

Hermit crabs are crabs that live in a snail shell. Like other crabs, they have a hard shell on the front half of their bodies, but, unlike other crabs, their back half is soft. Therefore, they have to borrow an empty snail shell to protect themselves. They twist the back parts of their bodies to fit into the snail shells. When they grow too large for the shell, they just leave it behind and find a larger one.

Like other crabs, hermit crabs have two pinchers as their front legs. They use these pinchers to grab or cut their food. Hermit crabs are scavengers, eating whatever food they can find lying around the tide pool. They often eat leftover food from other animals' meals or eat pieces of algae. They are very fast and can run away from predators.

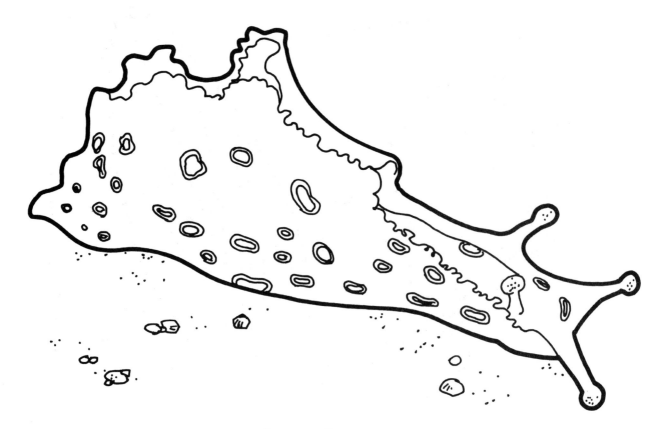

Sea Hare

The sea hare is a type of slug or a snail without a shell. The sea hare has a soft body and two antennae that look like rabbit ears. It has a strong muscular foot that it uses to hang on to the rocks while it crawls along eating algae in the tide pools. Some sea hares can grow to be larger than a football, while others are only 2 inches long.

Some sea hares live in tide pools, while others live in shallow waters off shore, away from the crashing waves. When it is in danger the sea hare squirts out ink that has a bad taste. This helps it to escape from its predators.

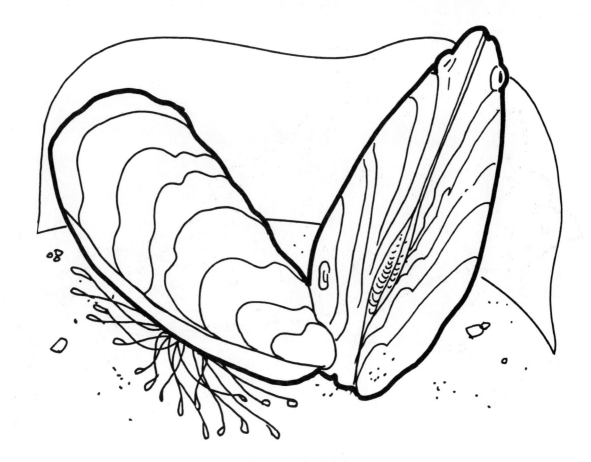

Mussel

The mussel is related to the snail, but instead of having its shell on its back, the mussel has two shells that close around its soft body. Even though mussels have two hard black or purple shells, there are other animals (like sea stars) that eat them. The mussel uses its foot to keep its shell closed when it is out of the water.

The mussel spends its life anchored to rocks by threads, called byssal threads, that it makes. When you find one mussel, you will most likely find many. Mussels like to cluster together to protect themselves from the pounding waves. If they break off a rock, they can make new byssal threads and attach to a new rock.

Mussels eat by filtering water over their gills and catching small plankton. Many other animals live in between the clumps of mussels.

Barnacle

Barnacles are small animals that attach themselves to a hard surface and stay there all their lives. The barnacle is related to a crab and has jointed legs that it uses to capture tiny plankton in the water. It also protects itself by making several hard plates around it that look like a volcano.

Barnacles are often found on rocks, boats, and piers. Other kinds of barnacles attach themselves to whales and travel the oceans along with their whale host. When baby barnacles are first born they float around in the ocean as plankton. When they are bigger they settle down on a hard surface and glue their head down. Once they are attached, they are ready to build their protective plates. The barnacles' hard outer plates protect them from the crashing waves, the hot sun, and predators.

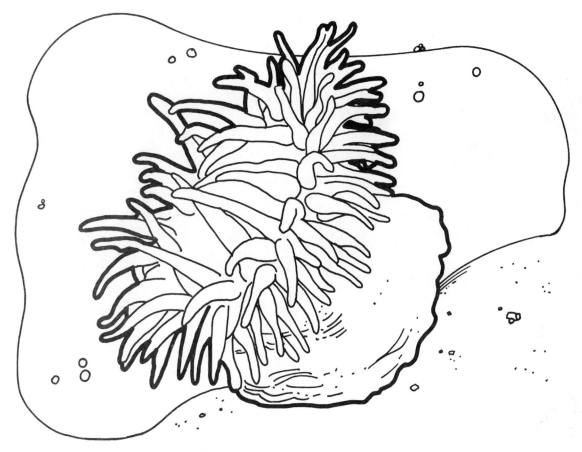

Sea Anemone

The sea anemone looks like a flower in the tide pool. It is very colorful and has several rows of tentacles surrounding its mouth. Sea anemones live in tide pools and often cover the outside of their bodies with small pieces of sand and shells to help protect themselves against the sun and predators.

Sea anemones are related to jellyfish, but they spend their lives attached to rocks. The sea anemone has stingers in its tentacles just like a jellyfish, but they are too small to hurt humans. Unlike the barnacle, the sea anemone can move, but it moves very, very slowly.

Sea anemones eat anything that they can catch in their stinger-filled tentacles. They often eat plankton, small crabs and any other organisms that might fall into their reach.

The sea anemone is a very simple animal. It does not have eyes, a brain, ears, a heart, or any complex organs. Some sea anemones can divide in half to make a new animal.

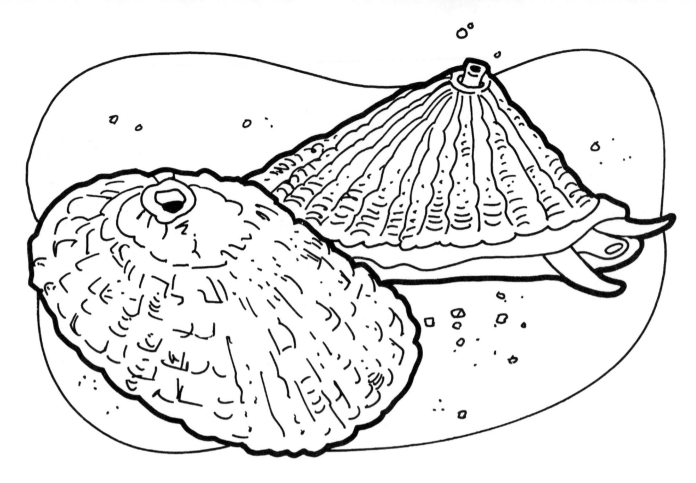

Limpet

The limpet is like a snail, but has a shell shaped like a flat cone. It belongs to a group of animals called mollusks. Other mollusks are snails, clams, mussels, oysters, octopuses, and squids. Limpets can be as small as a pencil eraser or as large as a dinner plate.

The limpet is also found on the rocks of the tide pool. If you don't look carefully you will not find this animal. It holds on tightly to the rock with its muscular foot and makes sure its shell fits tightly against the rock. The limpet eats algae around the tide pool by scraping it off with its rough tongue called a radula. Some limpets attach to seaweed and kelp.

Some limpets have a hole in the top of their shell. These are called key-hole limpets.

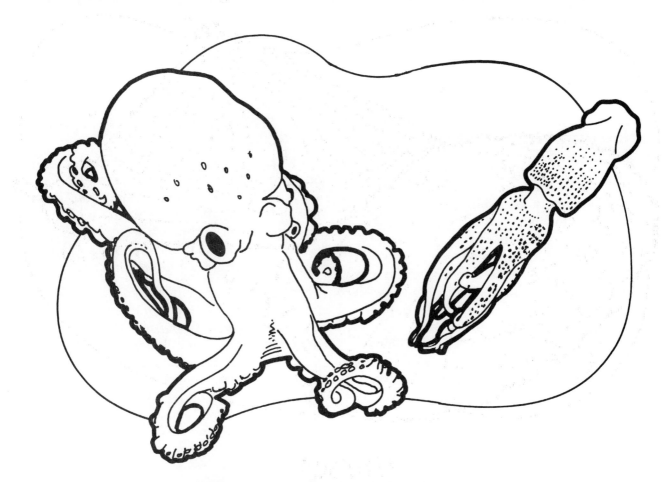

Octopus and Squid

Octopuses and squids are mollusks, like snails and clams. They do not, however, have shells. Octopuses have sac-like bodies with eight legs or tentacles. Squids also have soft bodies, but they have a small thin plate inside their body. They have ten tentacles, two of which are longer that the others. The tentacles have powerful suction cups on them. They use the tentacles to catch clams, crabs, lobsters and other shellfish that they eat.

Many octopus are small (about the size of your hand), but some are very large (32 feet or 10 meters long). Squids also can be very small (the size of your finger), but the giant squid can be 65 feet (20 meters) long.

Squids and octopuses are some of the smartest invertebrate animals. They have large brains and sharp eyes. They can change their body shape and color to hide from their enemies. When an octopus or a squid is in danger, it can also squirt out a dark liquid that hides it from the animal that is trying to capture it.

Food Chains
Building Connections in the Environment

Background Information
What is a Food Chain?

Every animal has to eat to survive, and most animals run the risk of being eaten themselves. A food chain is the transfer of energy, with each organism eating the member below it. Food chains and food webs are tools scientists use to look at the interactions between animals and plants. A food chain looks at a linear relationship between a small set of organisms, in which each animal only eats one other animal. A food web is a more complex, but realistic way of showing the relationship between many organisms that have a variety of food sources. For the purpose of this book and at this age level, we will simply look at food chains.

Producers and Consumers

A food chain always starts with the primary producer. A **primary producer** is a plant or algae that uses the sun's energy to make its own food through the process of photosynthesis. The primary producer does not have to eat anything to get energy; it makes it. An example of a primary producer is grass.

Next in the food chain comes the **primary consumer**. This is the animal that eats the primary producer. Primary consumers are herbivores. An example of a primary consumer is a deer.

Next consumers in the food chain are the **secondary** and **tertiary consumers**. The secondary consumer eats the primary consumer, and the tertiary consumer eats the secondary consumer. These animals are carnivores and omnivores (animals that eat plants and animals). An example is a mountain lion.

There may be many organisms in a food chain, each one adding to the length of the chain. Once you have constructed a food chain you can see the relationship of the organisms. Using this visual depiction, you can also hypothesize what would happen to the other organisms if one organism were removed from the food chain. In both a food chain and a food web, arrows are drawn from an organism to another organism that eats it.

Chapter Contents
This chapter is designed to introduce young students to food chains and show them how a balanced environment is dependent on having organisms at all levels of the food chain. The concepts presented in each lesson are:

7.1 - Basic concepts of food chains

7.2 - Construction of an ocean food chain

7.3 - Construction of three different food chains

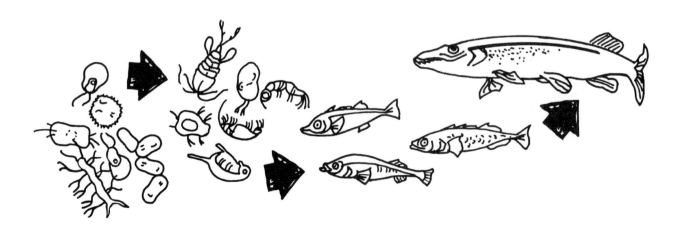

Food Chain
Activities

7.1 Food Chain

Overview

In this lesson students will examine the relationships between a few familiar animals.

Materials

- ✓ "Food Chains" worksheet
- ✓ pencil

Procedure

1. Introduce the concepts of food chains, pointing out how animals eat plants and other animals. Show a couple of examples by drawing pictures on the board and using arrows to indicate what each animal eats.

2. Give each student a copy of the worksheet.

3. Instruct them to draw an arrow that points from each organism to the animal that eats it (prey → predator).

7.2 Ocean Food Chain

Overview

In this lesson students will use their combined knowledge of the ocean and food chains to create an ocean food chain. This activity can be an individual activity or can become a bulletin board display.

Materials

- ✓ "Ocean Food Chain" worksheet
- ✓ scissors
- ✓ paste or string

Procedure

1. The worksheet has pictures of fish, an orca, phytoplankton, and zooplankton. Copy and distribute the pictures to the students.

2. Have each student cut apart and arrange the pictures to make a food chain.

3. You can have the students string them together or paste them onto a piece of paper.

7.3 What's for Dinner?

Overview

In this lesson students will create three different food chins.

Materials

- ✓ "What's for Dinner?" worksheet
- ✓ scissors
- ✓ glue

Procedure

1. Discuss the food chains that were made in the first two lessons. Also talk about what some of the marine animals that you have studied eat.

2. Make a sample food chain using some of the animals that you have discussed.

3. Give students the worksheet and have them cut out the pictures, arrange them to make three different food chains, and glue the pictures on another piece of paper.

4. Select animals from each food chain and discuss what would happen if this animal were to disappear (become extinct, move to a new location, etc.). What would happen to the other two animals in the food chain?

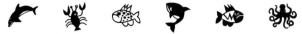

If You Live by the Ocean

If you live by the ocean you have the ideal opportunity to observe an ocean food chain. If you take your class to the beach have them find an animal such as a sea bird. See if they can find what the bird is eating. Repeat the process with as many animals as you can find.

Follow-Up Questions/Activities

- Talk about what would happen if one of the animals were taken out of a food chain. What would happen to the other animals? Would some animals lower on the food chain not have any more predators and increase in numbers? Would other animals not have anything to eat?

- See if your students can come up with their own food chain from animals that live around them. Have them draw pictures of these animals with arrows showing which animals eat the other animals.

- What if all animals were plant eaters (herbivores)?

- Make a food chain mobile with each level representing a different level of the food chain.

Food Chains

Name _____

Draw an arrow to show what each thing eats.

Example

1.

2.

3.

4.

Ocean Food Chain

Name _____

Cut out the pictures. Arrange them to make a food chain. Glue the pictures
on another piece of paper.

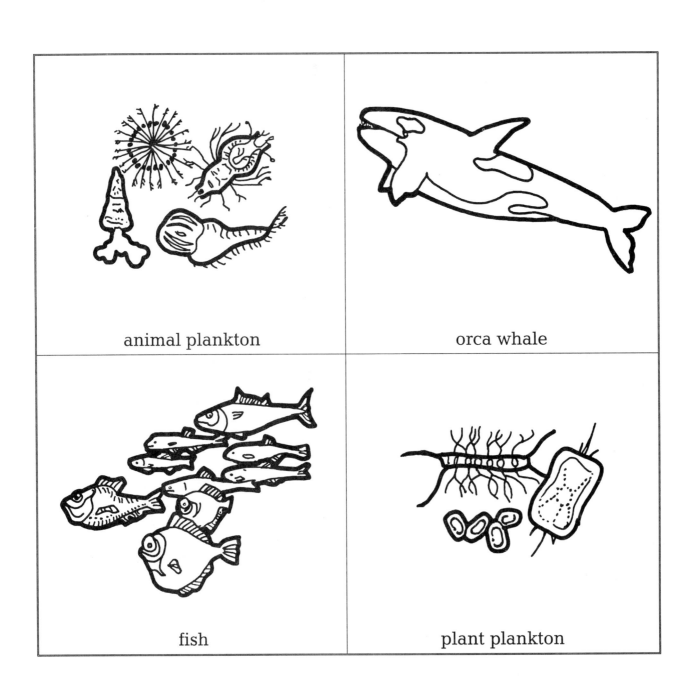

animal plankton

orca whale

fish

plant plankton

What's for Dinner?

Name _____

Cut out the pictures and arrange them into three different food chains. Glue the pictures in the correct order on another piece of paper.

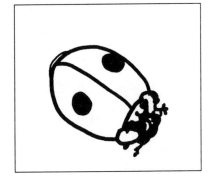

Glossary

Adaptation - changes in an organism with respect to its environment

Algae - a group of simple, plant-like organism that use chlorophyll in photosynthesis; they occur in fresh or salt water

Antennae - movable sensory appendages occurring in pairs on the head of organisms

Baleen - an elastic, horny substance growing in place of teeth in the upper jaw of certain whales and forming a series of thin, parallel plates

Blowhole - the opening on the top of a whale or dolphin through which it breathes

Blubber - the thick layer of fat that insulates marine mammals

Byssal threads - strong, horny threads by which the animal attaches to the substrate

Camouflage - the act, art, or means of disguising things to deceive an enemy

Carapace - a shield covering some or all of the dorsal part of an animal

Carnivore - an animal that feeds primarily on other animals

Cartilage - a firm, elastic, flexible type of connective tissue

Consumers - organisms in a food chain that get their energy by eating plants and other animals

Crustacean - a group of animals with jointed appendages and a hard exoskeleton; includes crabs, lobsters, shrimp, and barnacles

Echolocation - the detection of an object by reflected sound; used by marine mammals

Ecology - the study of the relationships among organisms and their environment

Ecosystem - an environmental unit that consists of living and nonliving parts

Environment - the external surroundings of an organism

Erosion - the breaking down of sediment and rocks by moving water

Estuary - a marshy inlet of the ocean where it meets the end of a river

Evaporate - to change a liquid or solid into vapor; to remove the water from a substance

Exoskeleton - a hard external skeleton covering an invertebrate such as a crab

Filter feeding - a means of attaining food by filtering it out of the water using specialized appendages or organs

Fin - an appendage of fish and fish-like animals; used for moving through water, steering, and balancing

Flippers - the pectoral fins of marine mammals

Fluke - the caudal fin of a whale or dolphin

Gills - the breathing organisms of aquatic animals through which the animals get oxygen from the water

Habitat - the living place (home) of one specific organism; characterized by its physical and biological properties

Herbivore - an animal that feeds on plants

Krill - a shrimp-like organism than occurs in dense swarms in polar waters; the main food of some whales

Invertebrate - a animal without a backbone

Mammal - a large group of warm-blooded vertebrates in which the females have milk-secreting glands and give live birth

Molting - the shedding of the exoskeleton in crustaceans such as crabs

Ocean currents - the movement of large masses of water in river-like patterns in the world's oceans

Omnivore - an animal that eats both plants and animals

Operculum - a round hard or horny lid that closes when a snail retreats into its shell

Organism - any form of plant or animal life

Phytoplankton - photosynthetic plankton; plant plankton

Plankton - aquatic organisms that drift with water movement; usually very small

Predators - an animal that obtains energy (food) by killing and eating another organism

Primary producers - any plant or algae that uses the sun's energy for photosynthesis to produce its own nourishment

Salinity - a measure of the total number of dissolved solids in water; measured in parts per thousand in weight

Scavenger - an animal that eats refuse and decaying matter

Species - a group of organisms that resembles each other closely and that can reproduce

Temperate - the areas between the tropics and poles with moderate water temperature and weather

Tentacles - long, slender, flexible structures used for grasping or moving

Tide - the periodic rise and fall of the oceans water due to the gravitational pull of the moon and sun

Tide pool - areas of the rocky coast where pools are formed in rock depressions during low tide

Tropical - a warm area between the Tropic of Cancer and Tropic of Capricorn

Tube-feet - hollow tubes, many with suction cups, used for locomotion in sea stars, sea urchins and similar animals

Vertebrate - an animal with a backbone

Zooplankton - animal plankton

Answers

Tide Pool Treasures, page 16
Answers will vary, but all animals should be animals that actually live in tide pools.

Graphing the Earth, page 21
Check for correct coloring.
Most of the earth is covered with oceans.

Water Words, page 24

fresh water	salt water
drink	don't drink
lake	ocean
frog	whale
water lily	seaweed
	shark

Other answers will vary.

Getting to Know a Fish, page 31

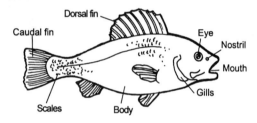

Fish Shapes, page 32
Fast swimming - tuna (top picture)
Lives on the sand - halibut (bottom picture)
Eats food in the cracks - long nose butterfly fish (middle picture)

Getting to Know a Whale, page 38

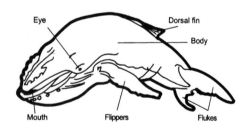

Marine Mammals and Me, page 39

person	seal
has hair	has hair
breathes air	breathes air
lives on land	lives in the ocean
baby drinks milk	baby drinks milk
has hands	fast swimmer
eats fish	eats fish
has bones	has bones
has a warm body	has a warm body

Invertebrates and Me, page 51

person	octopus
eyes	eyes
bones	soft body
lives on land	lives in the water
hands	tentacles
brain	brain
apples	fish
fish	suction cups
heart	heart

Backbones or No Backbones, page 52

vertebrates	invertebrates
bird	squid
fish	sea star
deer	snail
whale	hermit crab
snake	worm

Food Chains, page 67
1. grass → deer
2. person ← apple
3. grass → deer → wolf
4. grain → chicken → person

Ocean Food Chain, page 68

plant plankton
↓
animal plankton
↓
fish
↓
orca whale

What's for Dinner, page 69
sea urchin → sea otter → orca whale
plants → small fish → shark
leaf → insect → bird